FLIP-FLOP

AC128 Transistor
100μF (16 volt working) Electrolytic Capacitor
10K (brown/black/brown) Resistor
Indicator Bulb, 6 volt, 0.04 amp
Connecting Wire

AUDIO OSCILLATOR

2 of 0.1μF Disc Capacitor
10μF (16 volt working) Electrolytic Capacitor
Crystal Earpiece
2 of 1K (black/brown/red) Resistor
2 of 22K (red/red/orange) Resistor

MORSE CODE OSCILLATOR

4.7K (yellow/purple/red) Resistor
0.1μF Disc Capacitor

ONE 'POT' VIOLIN

50K (Linear) Potentiometer

PHOTOPHON

ORP 12 Light dependent Resistor

ELECTRONIC ORGAN

8 of 50K (or 47K) Pre-set Resistors
16 of No. 8 Screws and Screwcups
Cooking Foil

AMPLIFIER

AC128 Transistor
33K (orange/orange/orange) Resistor
10K (black/brown/orange) Resistor
1K (black/brown/red) Resistor
10μF (16 volt) Electrolytic Capacitor
100μF (16 volt) Electrolytic Capacitor
Eagle LT700 Output Transformer
Small 3Ω (or 8Ω) Loudspeaker

VIBRATO

Transistor
2 volt) Electrolytic Capacitor
d/violet/red) Resistor
own/black/orange) Resistor
/black/yellow)

We live in an electronics age with space satellites, moon landings, computers, etc. You might think that these are very complicated but they are all based on some quite simple electronic circuits. This book describes and explains in words and pictures some of these basic components that make up the miracles of our present-day life. Children will be able to make electric organs and violins, flip-flop circuits for sound and light and a variety of other exciting pieces of electronic wizardry. All the components are readily available and the equipment needed to build the circuits is simple and as inexpensive as possible. This makes it possible for youngsters to enjoy all the excitement of making and using the circuits and learning something about electronics at the same time.

Simple Electronics

by REV GEORGE C DOBBS

illustrated by ROLAND BERRY

Ladybird Books Loughborough

Look around your home and see how many electronic items you have in everyday use. You may find a television set, radio set, a record player, a cassette recorder and perhaps other electronic devices: all of them a part of your everyday life. Yet only a hundred years ago there were none of these things. The growth of electronics, from a few simple laboratory experiments to the amazing modern world of electronic devices, has been called the miracle of the century. You can learn something of this miracle by reading the Ladybird book *The Story of Radio*.

Electronic devices look very complex: a mass of wires, small parts and controls; but it is possible using a few inexpensive components to explore this world for yourself. This book will enable a complete beginner to carry out simple electronic experiments, and at the same time to build up some interesting little projects.

The world of electronics is wide, and covers many types of apparatus. This simple book is merely a door into that world, but the reader will learn enough to be able to follow up this fascinating subject, which can become a life-long hobby or even a future career!

This book does not deal with the building of radio receivers; this facet of electronics may be explored using the Ladybird book *Making a Transistor Radio*. That book also provides much of the background material which will help the reader to follow the projects described in this book.

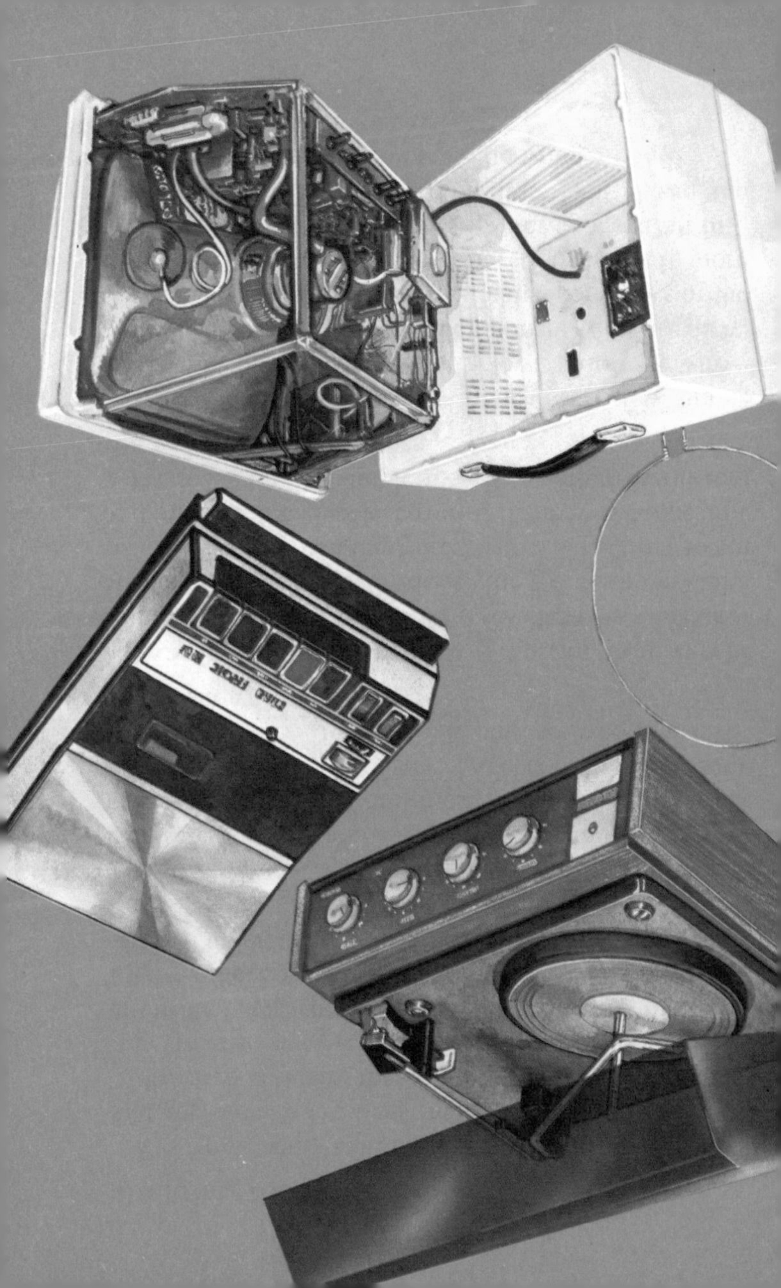

Building the projects

Electronic equipment is made up of *electronic circuits*, and the circuits are constructed from the parts called *components*. Usually the components are soldered into the circuits, but we shall use a simple method of electronics construction called "breadboard mounting", used in the early days of radio. The components are screwed down to a wooden board. A full explanation of this method is given on pages 14 to 17 of *Making a Transistor Radio*. The components are held down and connected using No. 6 brass screwcups and No. 6 brass screws, obtainable from most hardware shops. The baseboard for most of the projects is a 6in (15cm) length of $2\frac{3}{4}$in × $\frac{1}{2}$in (7cm × 1.3cm) softwood, marked out as shown.

Very few tools are required – most of them can be found in any home toolbox. A bradawl or gimlet for starting the holes, a screwdriver for No. 6 screws and a pair of pliers for bending wires, with a side-cutter to cut and remove the plastic covering from the connecting wires, make up our simple toolkit. Another useful tool is a wirecutter and stripper.

When building the circuits remember a few simple tips. Screw the screwcups firmly down onto bare wire – not the plastic coating. If the component wires are dirty, scrape them clean. Do not over-tighten the screws or the wood will tear, making the connection loose. If more than one wire is to be held by a screwcup, put all into place before making the connection tight. Keep the screws as straight as possible in the wood.

CIRCUIT BASEBOARD

Screwcup

Lead

Board

TOOLS REQUIRED

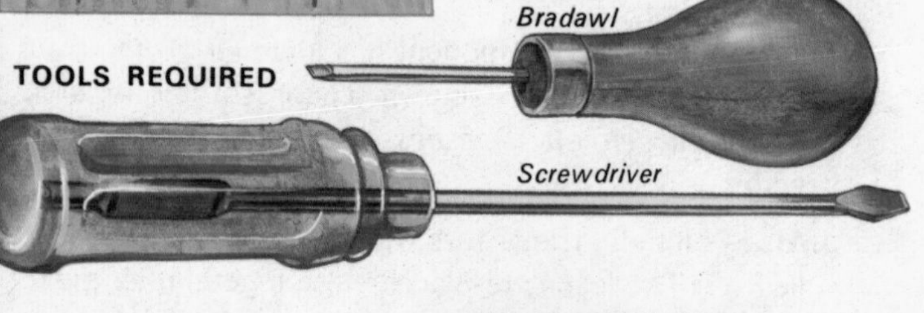

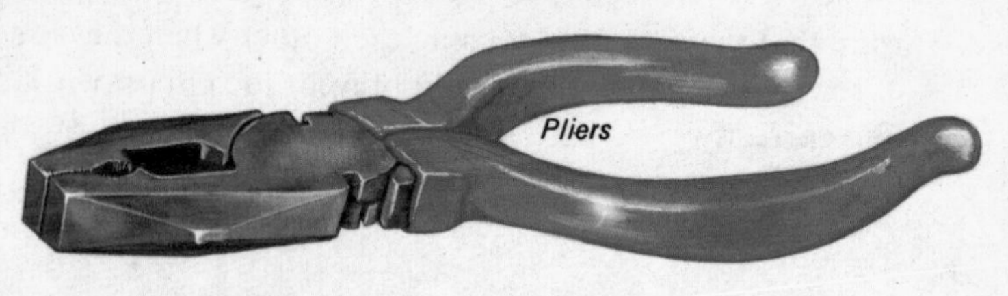

Electronic components – the transistor

All of the electronic components used in this book are easy to obtain, either from a local radio dealer, or usually more cheaply, from specialist electronics supply shops. If the components are difficult to obtain locally, all the popular electronic monthly magazines contain advertisements for mail order firms which will supply the components.

The main component in the projects is the *transistor*. The transistor is a small electronic device which has taken the place of the valve used in older electronic equipment. There are many types of transistor available. The transistor used in these projects is coded AC128.

The transistor can be used as an amplifier (that is, to make electronic signals stronger – see page 28, *Making a Transistor Radio*) but we are going to use it as an electronic switch. The transistor has three leads called the *emitter*, *base* and *collector*. The correct connections for the AC128 are shown in the drawing. **Always connect these leads in the correct position** or you may damage the transistor.

Every electronic component has a *circuit symbol*; the symbol for a transistor is shown. These symbols are used to make the *circuit diagrams* used in electronic construction.

Always handle transistors with care: the leads can be pulled off. The leads are placed close together, so make sure that they are not touching each other when they are screwed into place: this would prevent the circuit working correctly.

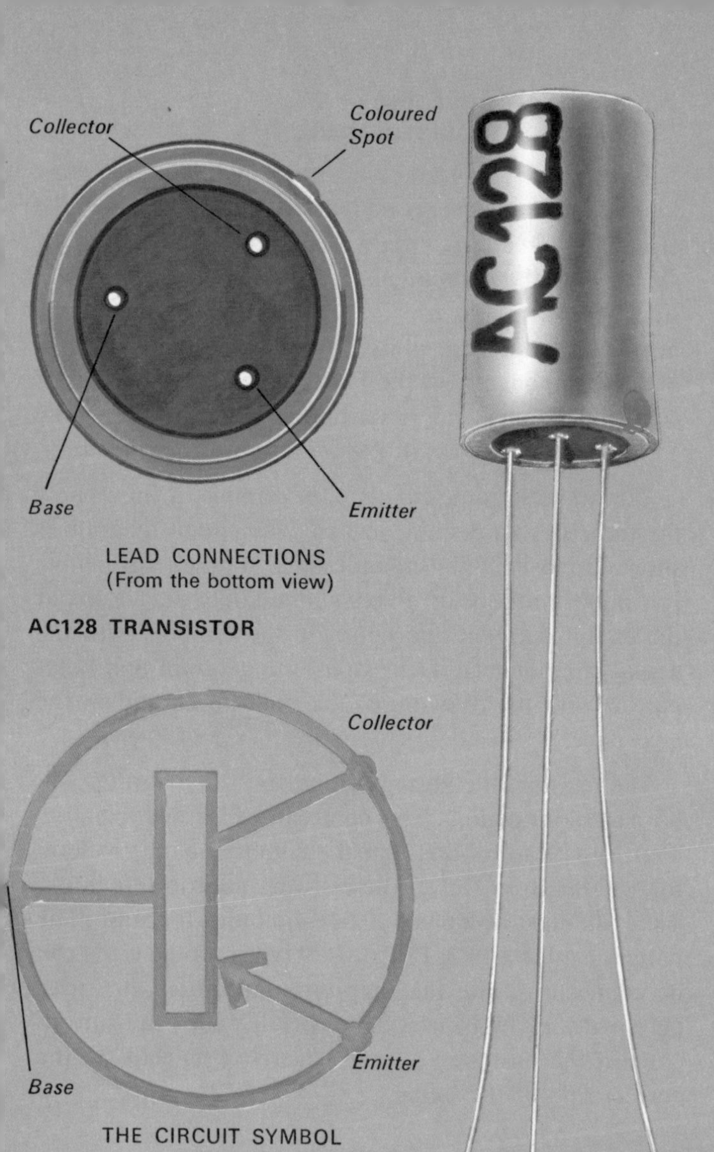
Collector
Coloured Spot
Base
Emitter
LEAD CONNECTIONS
(From the bottom view)
AC128 TRANSISTOR
Collector
Emitter
Base
THE CIRCUIT SYMBOL
AC128
e
b
c

An electronic circuit – the simple transistor switch

Electronics engineers use circuit diagrams to show how the components are connected together to make the electronic circuit. A circuit diagram is like a map. It shows how the components are joined electrically, but since the symbols are joined by straight lines for neatness, it does not always show the actual positions of the components on the board. A full explanation of circuit diagrams and descriptions of many electronic components are given in *Making a Transistor Radio*.

Our first electronic circuit is very simple. It shows how the transistor works as a switch. The circuit diagram is shown opposite, with the individual components below. It is important to learn to read circuit diagrams. Look at the circuit diagram and compare the symbols with the actual components. Then study the diagram and compare it with the drawing of the built-up circuit on the next page.

The resistor, the zigzag symbol on the diagram, will have a colour coding. This code can be learned from the Transistor Radio book, but the coloured bands to look for will be given for all the resistors used in this book. The bulb must be a 6 volt, 0.04 amp indicator lamp. The battery can be a PP3, PP7 or PP9 type and the leads can be connected using the snap-on connectors which can be bought, or by using small crocodile clips. Be sure to connect the positive (+) and negative (−) leads to the correct side of the battery.

THE TRANSISTOR SWITCH

CIRCUIT DIAGRAM

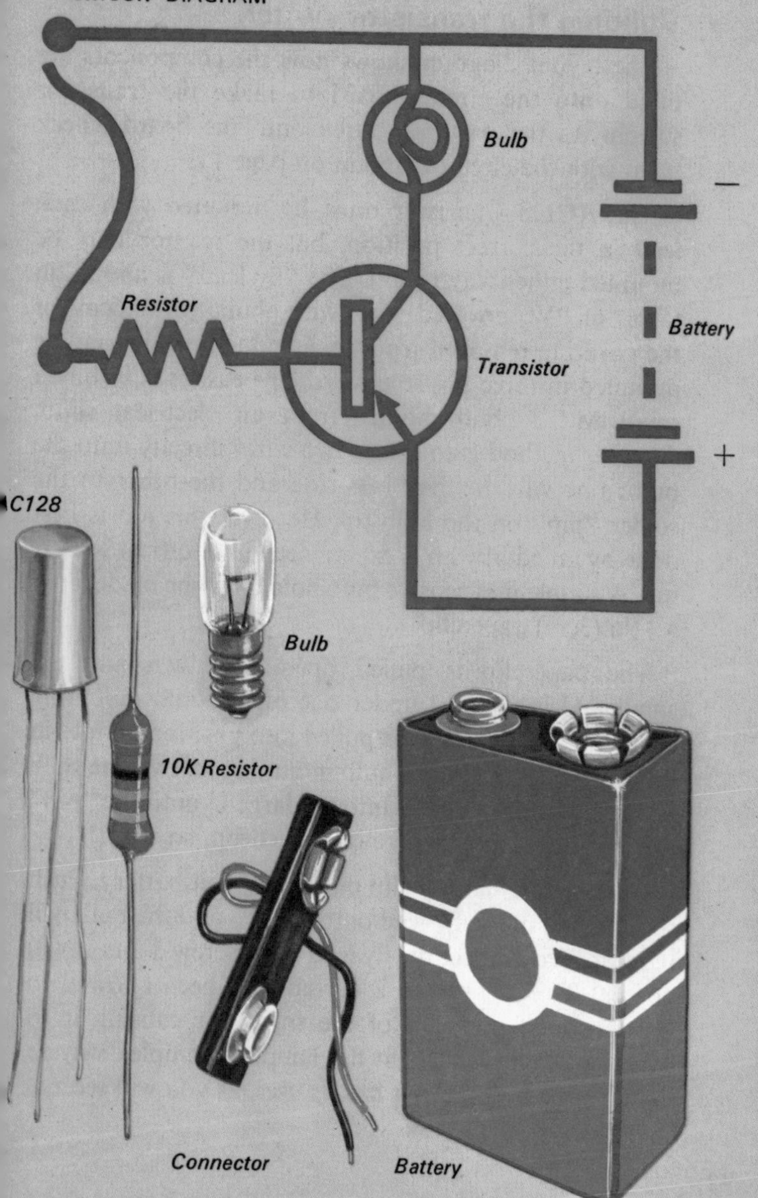

Building the transistor switch

The layout diagram shows how the components are fitted onto the circuit board to make the transistor switch. As the parts are fitted onto the board, check them with the circuit diagram on page 11.

The AC128 transistor must be mounted with each lead in the correct position, but the resistor may be mounted either way round. The "fly lead" is about 2in (5cm) of PVC covered wire, with about $\frac{1}{4}$in (0.6cm) of the covering removed from each end. The bulb may be mounted in three possible ways. The easiest is to buy a small M.E.S. bulb holder from an electrical shop. Another method is to solder two wires directly onto the bulb; one wire to the brass side and the other to the solder "pip" on the bulb tip. However this job is best done by an adult who is experienced in electrical soldering. A simple inexpensive bulb holder can be made from a 1$\frac{1}{4}$in (3cm) paperclip.

The paperclip is pulled open as shown and the smaller U is screwed under one of the bulb mounting screwcups. The large U is pulled into position about $\frac{1}{4}$in (0.6cm) above the other bulb mounting screw. The bulb is then carefully screwed into the large U until the "pip" touches the screw. Paperclips are cheap, so try it!

Connect the battery clip onto the 9 volt battery. Push the free end of the fly lead onto screw 3 and the bulb will light up. Disconnect the fly lead from screw 3 and it will go out. This is because a current has been allowed to flow through the base of the transistor causing it to conduct heavily and light the lamp. A complex way to light a lamp? Yes, but it has its uses, as you will see.

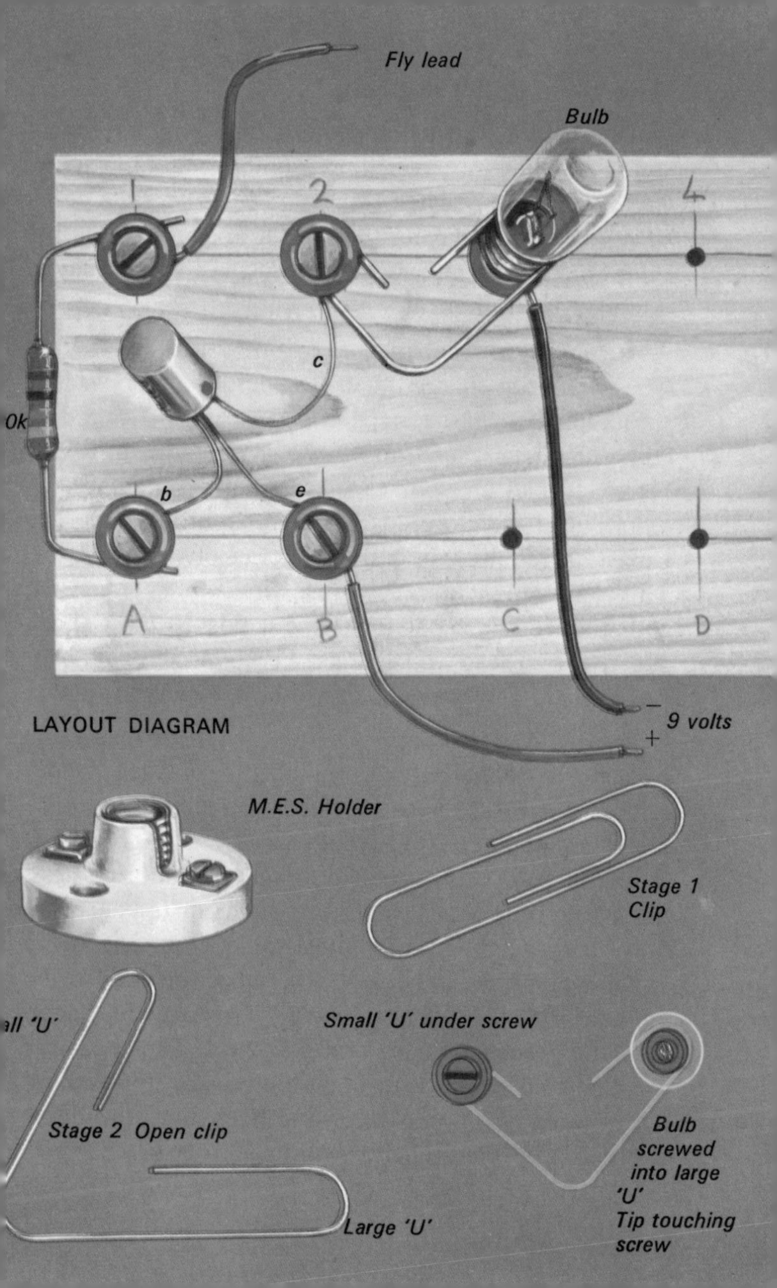
Fly lead
Bulb
1
2
4
Ok
c
b
e
A
B
C
D
− 9 volts +
LAYOUT DIAGRAM
M.E.S. Holder
Stage 1 Clip
all 'U'
Small 'U' under screw
Stage 2 Open clip
Bulb screwed into large 'U' Tip touching screw
Large 'U'

The time delay switch

The transistor switch appears to be a complex way of doing a simple job; switching a bulb on and off. However, a transistor switch can be used for several special jobs, including delaying the time it takes to switch the bulb onto full brightness. A time delay can be shown by adding one component – a capacitor.

A capacitor can be "charged up" with electricity. The amount of charge it will store and the time it takes to accept this charge, depend upon capacitance value. This value is measured in *farads*. The farad is too large for electronics and our capacitors will be measured in values of μF (microfarads or one millionth farads). The capacitor required is a 100μF electrolytic capacitor. This is a small metal tube with a wire coming from each end. Electrolytic capacitors have a positive (+) and a negative (−) lead which must be connected the right way round. The drawing shows how to identify them.

The fly lead is removed from the board and the capacitor is connected with the positive (+) lead under screwcup 1. Press the end of the negative (−) lead onto the screw number 2. The bulb will slowly light up. It should take about one second to light to full brightness, this is the time that it takes the capacitor to charge up fully and switch on the transistor. Before the delay switching can be repeated, the capacitor has to be "discharged". This can be done by "shorting" it, that is, touching the negative lead onto screw 1. The capacitor can also be discharged through the resistor by touching the negative lead onto screw A. Each time the delay switch is used the capacitor will have to be discharged.

TIME DELAY SWITCH

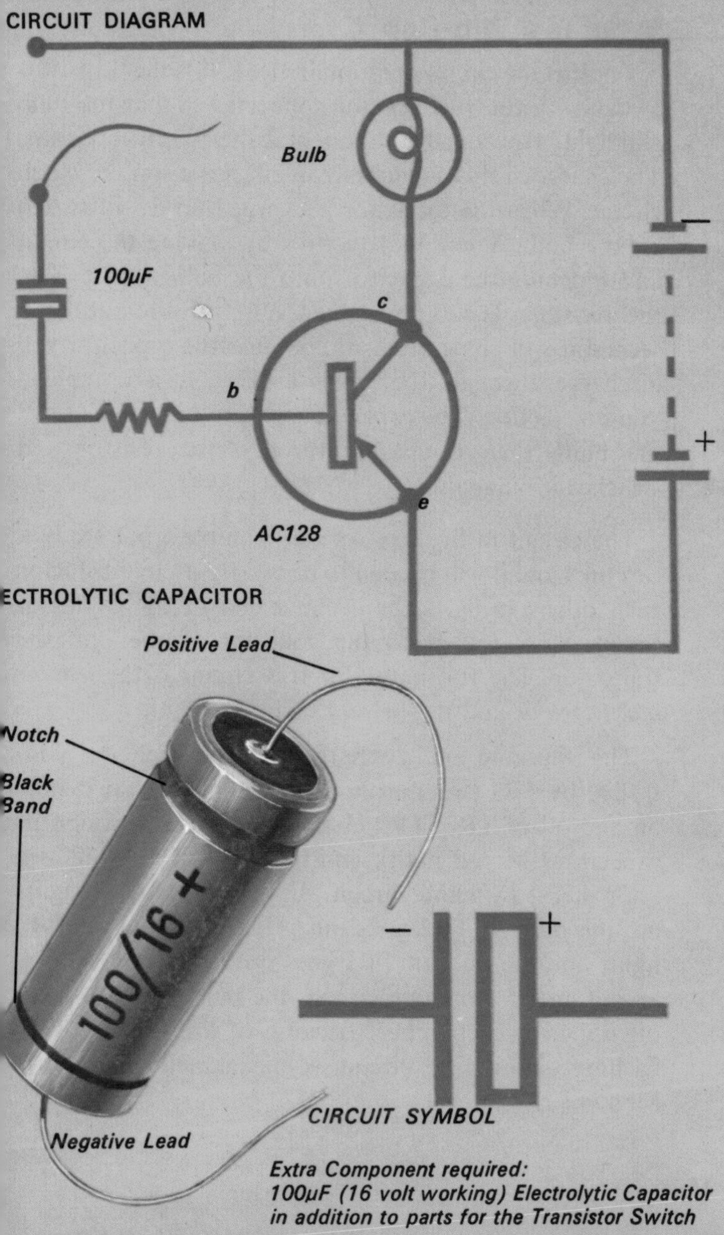

Extra Component required:
100μF (16 volt working) Electrolytic Capacitor in addition to parts for the Transistor Switch

What is a 'flip-flop'?

Look at the circuit diagram in fig. 1. It is the transistor switch with the 10K resistor connected so that the bulb will light. The added component is the 100µF capacitor. The charge in this capacitor can effect the simple switch circuit. When the capacitor is charged up it will switch off the bulb. You could try this by making the circuit and touching the capacitor onto the bulb (top) end of the resistor. The bulb will go off, but after about a second it will come on again, because the capacitor will discharge through the resistor. This is a combined "on-off" action. The capacitor charges up, switches off the bulb, then discharges through the resistor and switches it on again.

The circuit in fig. 2 looks very complex, but study it carefully and it will be seen to be two fig. 1 circuits facing each other. In fig. 2 the negative end of the capacitor (point X) is joined to the collector of the opposite transistor. The full name for this circuit is the *astable multivibrator* and it is a very cunning circuit.

The charging and discharging of the capacitor controlled by TR1 (the purple path) controls the switching on and off of TR2. TR2 at the same time, through its capacitor (the red path), controls TR1. The result is a "non-stop" switching circuit. As the bulb of TR1 lights up, the bulb of TR2 goes out – then the bulb of TR2 lights and the bulb of TR1 goes out and so on. This is an automatic switching circuit, the bulbs going on and off opposite each other. Because of this "swop-over" flashing action, the circuit is nicknamed "The Flip-Flop"

TRANSISTOR SWITCH

FIG. 1

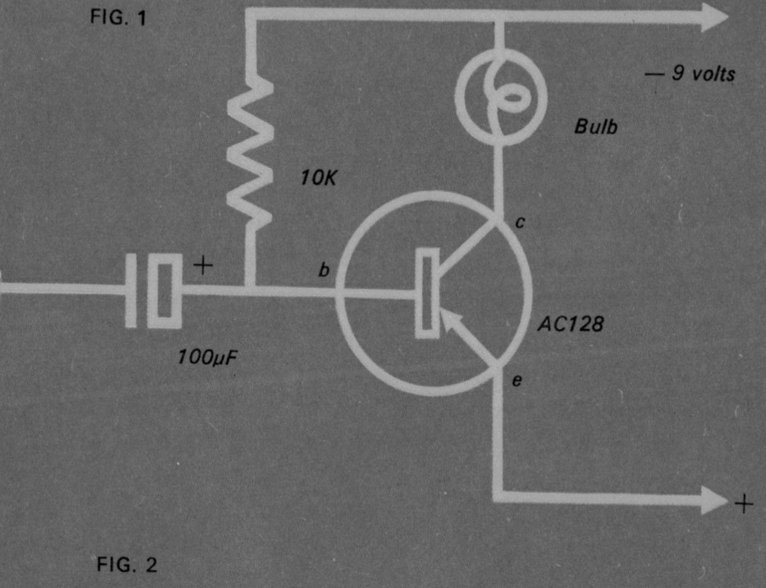

FIG. 2

FLIP-FLOP

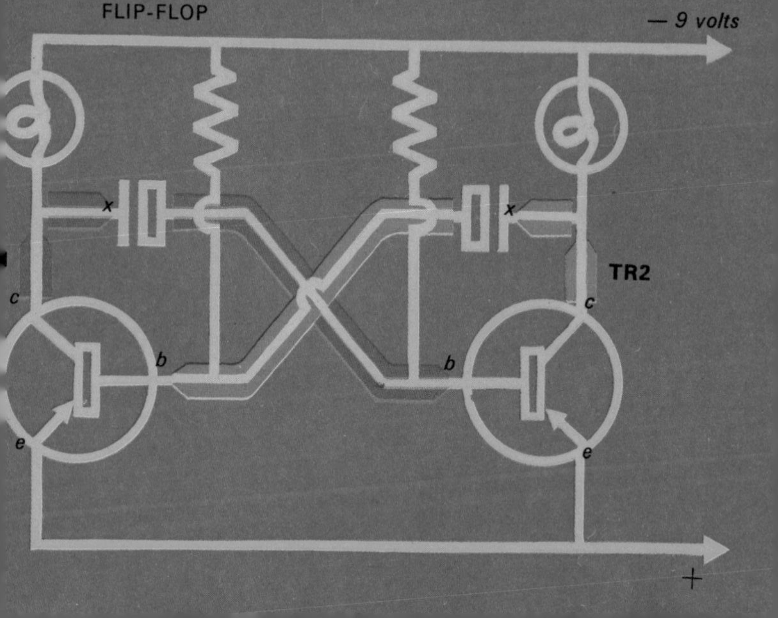

Making a flip-flop (1)

The flip-flop circuit is quite simple to build and the on-off switching of the lights make it great fun! The full circuit is shown in the drawing. It requires another set of the components used to build the time delay switch circuit. Study the circuit diagram carefully and compare it with the layout drawing over the page.

Since the circuit is twice as complex as the time delay switch, great care must be taken when building it on the board. The transistor leads must be connected correctly and then checked, remembering that the two transistors are connected with the base leads going towards the centre. The capacitors must also be connected the correct way round. Check that both positive leads are connected to the transistor base screws and the negative leads are connected to the transistor collector screws.

The circuit has to switch two bulbs on and off, so if it is to be used for any length of time a reasonable sized battery will be required. The small PP3 will not last for long in this circuit. The larger PP6 (or better still – the PP9) will run the circuit for quite some time. All of these are 9 volt batteries.

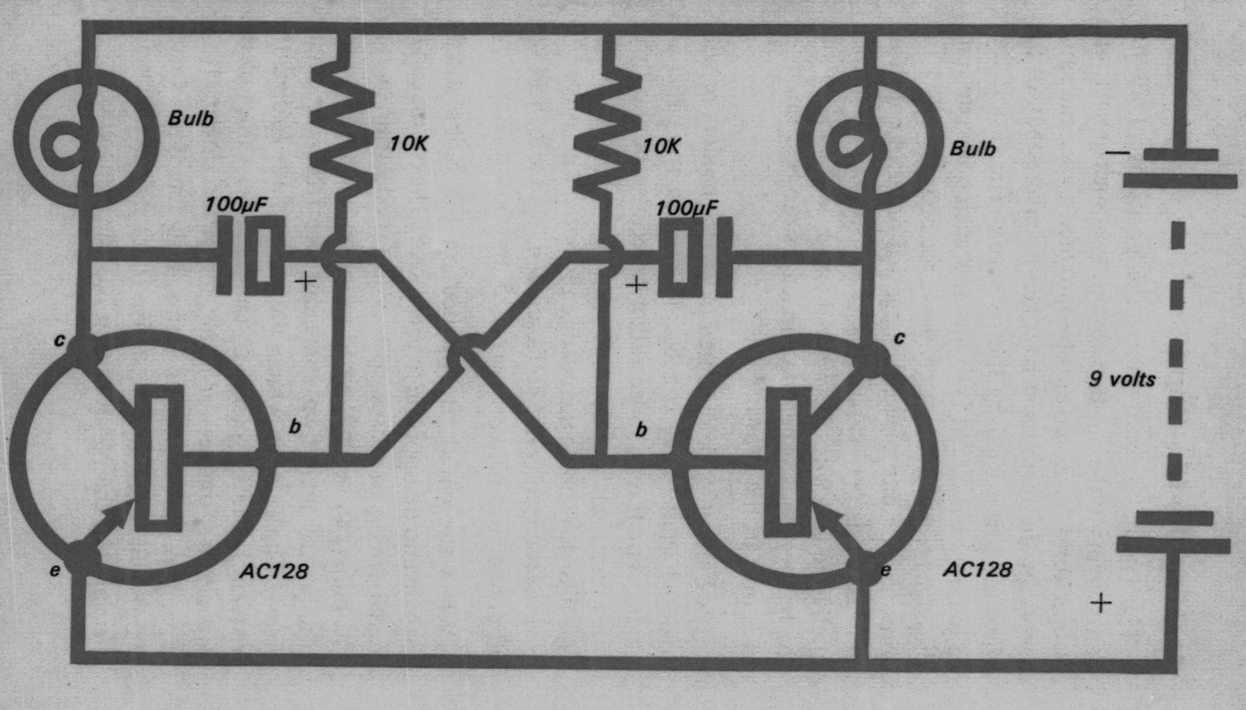
Bulb
10K
10K
Bulb
100µF
100µF
+
+
−
c
c
b
b
9 volts
e
e
AC128
AC128
+

Making the flip-flop (2)

The layout diagram shows the positions of all the components in the flip-flop circuit. In some connections, two or three wires have to be mounted under the same screwcup, and care must be taken to ensure that all the wires are firmly held by the screwcup. The easiest way to build up the circuit is to unscrew each screwcup until the edge is just high enough above the board to allow the wires to slide into place. A suggested order of construction is: resistors, capacitors, transistors, bulbs, then finally the two wires between B and E and 2 and 5 and the battery leads. The two capacitors are best mounted as shown in the drawing.

The bulbs may be mounted in M.E.S. holders or with soldered leads. They can be mounted in the paperclip holder, but this is more difficult because of the three wires under each of the screwcups on the top row. An on-off switch can be included in the battery negative (–) lead, or the lead could go to screw 6, with a fly lead on-off connection between screws 5 and 6.

When the circuit is switched on the bulbs should flash on and off opposite to each other. The circuit can be used for many purposes, such as on a model train layout. The bulbs can be on the end of longer wires and be put in a box of their own some distance from the circuit board. The rate at which the bulbs flash (called the frequency) can be altered by changing the values of the capacitors – smaller for faster, larger for slower. 10µF capacitors will make the bulbs flash ten times faster, 500µF will make them flash five times slower. Changing the value of the resistors also has the same effect.

AYOUT

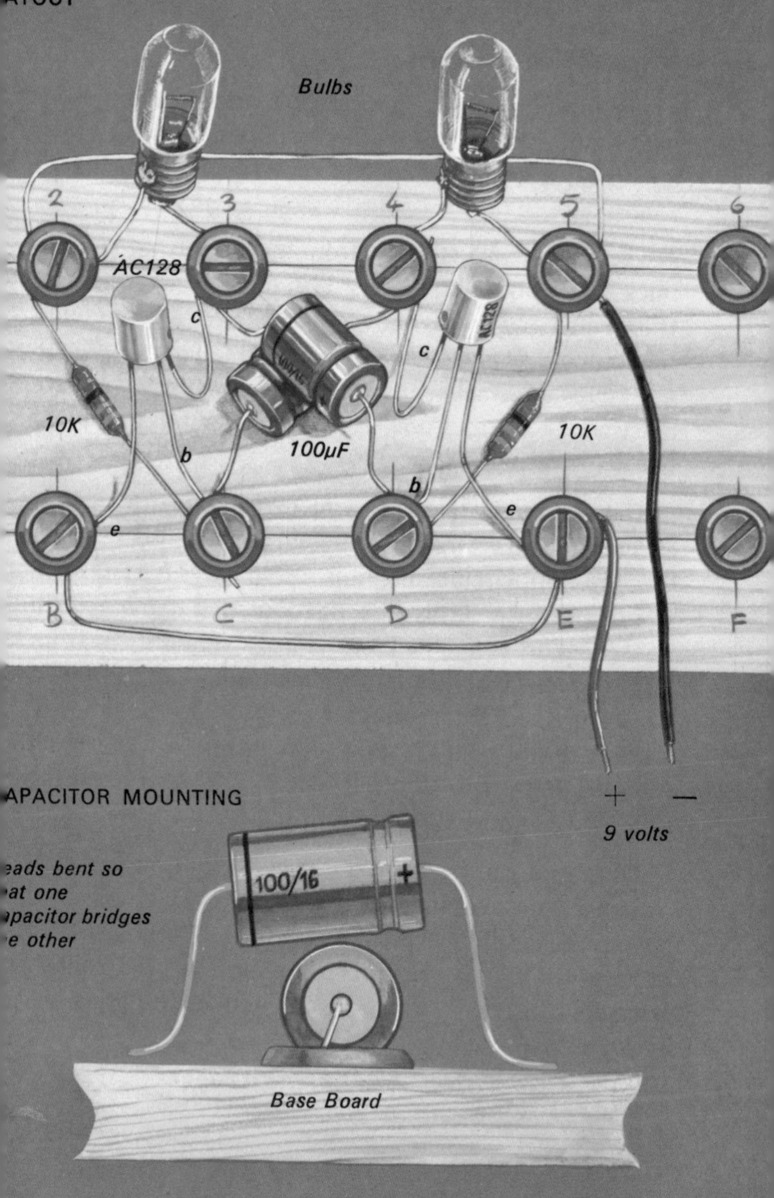

APACITOR MOUNTING

eads bent so
at one
apacitor bridges
e other

The flashing robot

The flip-flop light flasher can be used to make a robot with flashing eyes. This requires a different layout of the circuit on a smaller wooden board, cut to look like a robot.

The base board is made from a piece of $\frac{1}{2}$in (1.3cm) thick soft wood, 6in long by $1\frac{3}{4}$in (15cm $\times$ 4.4cm) wide. It is drilled and cut as shown, and 12 No. 8 screws and screwcups are placed at 1in (2.5cm) intervals. No. 8 screwcups are smaller than the No. 6 size, so extra care must be taken to put the screws in straight and hold all the wires firmly in place.

The robot is wired up as in the layout drawing. A check will show that this different layout also matches the flip-flop circuit diagram on page 17. The two transistors form "arms" for the robot, and to make them thicker, short pieces of PVC wire sleeving are cut from PVC covered wire to slip over the leads. The bulbs can be soldered to leads or screwed into M.E.S. holders. Take care not to allow any stray wires to touch each other as they cross. Connect to a 9 volt battery and the robot's eyes will flash on and off.

The robot can be given a "head" by placing a small plastic carton over the top of the board. Two holes will have to be cut in the carton to allow the "bulb eyes" to poke out. Or you may prefer to show all the robot's electronic "works" to show your skill at building the *electronic robot*.

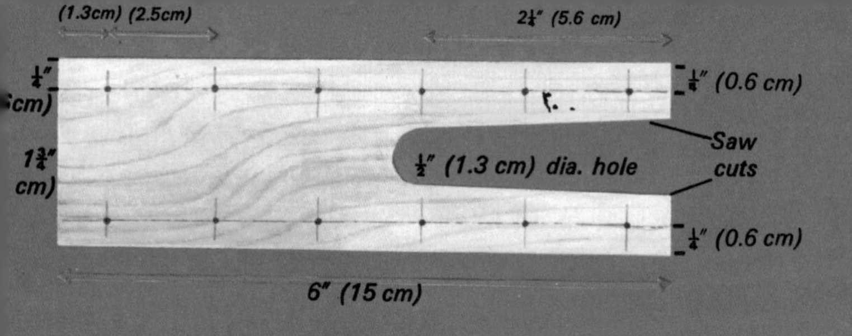

ROBOT CIRCUIT BOARD

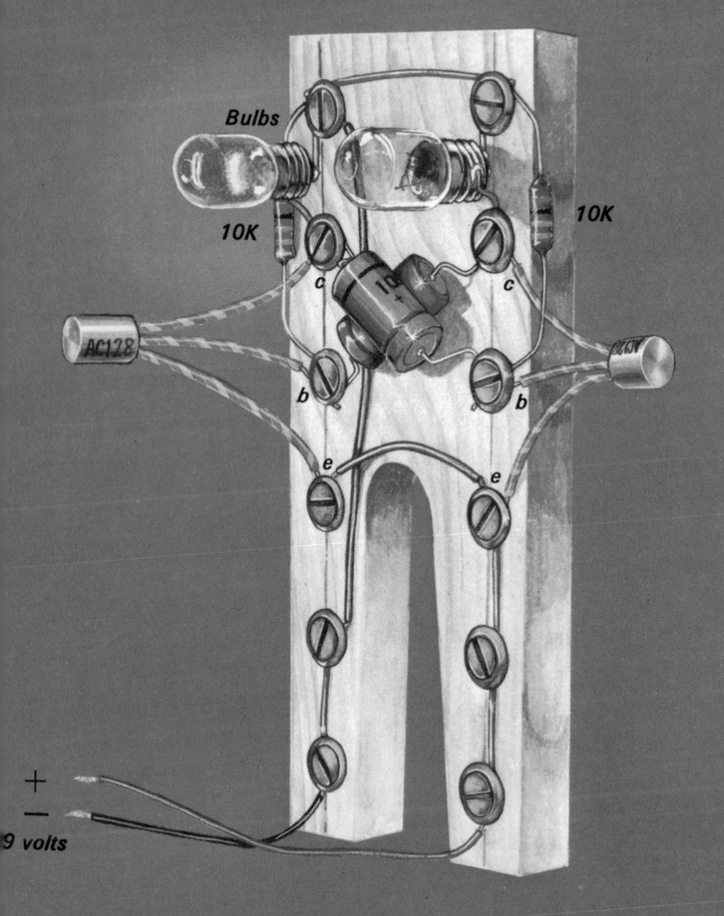

Making a noise!

The flip-flop is simply two transistors switching each other on and off, and the flashing lamps show this happening. It is a simple scientific fact that sound is caused by quick backward and forward movements, called vibrations or *oscillations*. For a more detailed explanation of this, you might like to read the Ladybird Book: *How it works – Television*. The rate at which the movement occurs is called the *frequency*. The flip-flop also has a sort of backward and forward movement (seen in the lamps) but these oscillations are too slow to produce a sound.

On page 20 it was mentioned that the rate of flashing of the lamps could be changed by altering the values of the capacitors and resistors. It is possible to do this so that the transistors switch too fast to flash lamps, but can be heard as a sound. They produce an *audio* (sound) signal. The circuit for this is shown in the drawing – note the capacitor values are much lower, the resistor values are higher and the bulbs have been replaced by two resistors. As this circuit is not to be 'looked at' but 'listened to', a 10μF capacitor takes the audio signal to a crystal earpiece. The earpiece is a *transducer*, that is, it turns the electrical audio waves into sound which we can hear.

The components are shown below the circuit. The earpiece must be a *crystal* type, not the common 'moving coil' type used for personal listening with transistor radios. The 0.1μF capacitor may be of any type, although the 'disc' types are more convenient for construction.

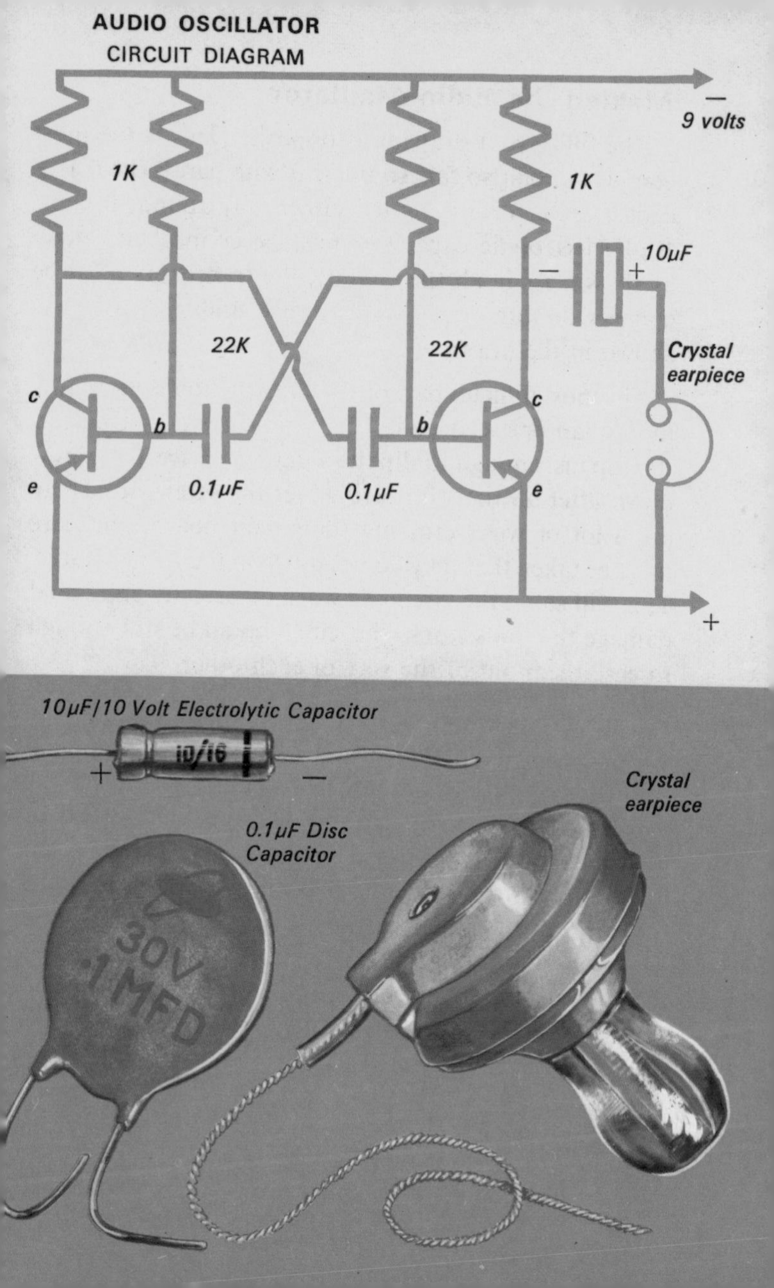
AUDIO OSCILLATOR
CIRCUIT DIAGRAM
—
9 volts
1K
1K
10μF
−
+
22K
22K
Crystal
earpiece
c
b
e
0.1μF
0.1μF
b
c
e
+
10μF/10 Volt Electrolytic Capacitor
10/16
+
—
Crystal
earpiece
0.1μF Disc
Capacitor
30V
·1MFD

Making the audio oscillator

The full layout drawing is opposite. This is the most complex circuit so far, so build it with care! The 0.1 μF capacitors can be mounted either way round, but the 10 μF electrolytic capacitor must be connected exactly as shown. As in all the circuits, the transistors must be connected with the correct leads under the screws shown in the drawing.

The most difficult part of the construction is mounting more than one lead under the same screwcup. Unscrew the cup just enough to slip the wires into place, and screw down after all the wires are under the screwcup. There are a lot of wires crossing the circuit board, and care must be taken that they do not touch in the wrong places. This will cause the circuit to work incorrectly and could damage the transistors. The wires should be stiff enough to ease them out of the way of each other.

Carefully check over the whole circuit for touching wires, check it against the layout drawing, and then against the circuit diagram. If it is correct connect the two leads to the 9 volt battery. Quite a loud sound of a single tone will be heard in the earpiece. It may be loud enough to hear without putting the earpiece into the ear. Most crystal earpieces have an earplug tube which will unscrew. If this is unscrewed and taken off, the sound should be clear some distance away from the earpiece.

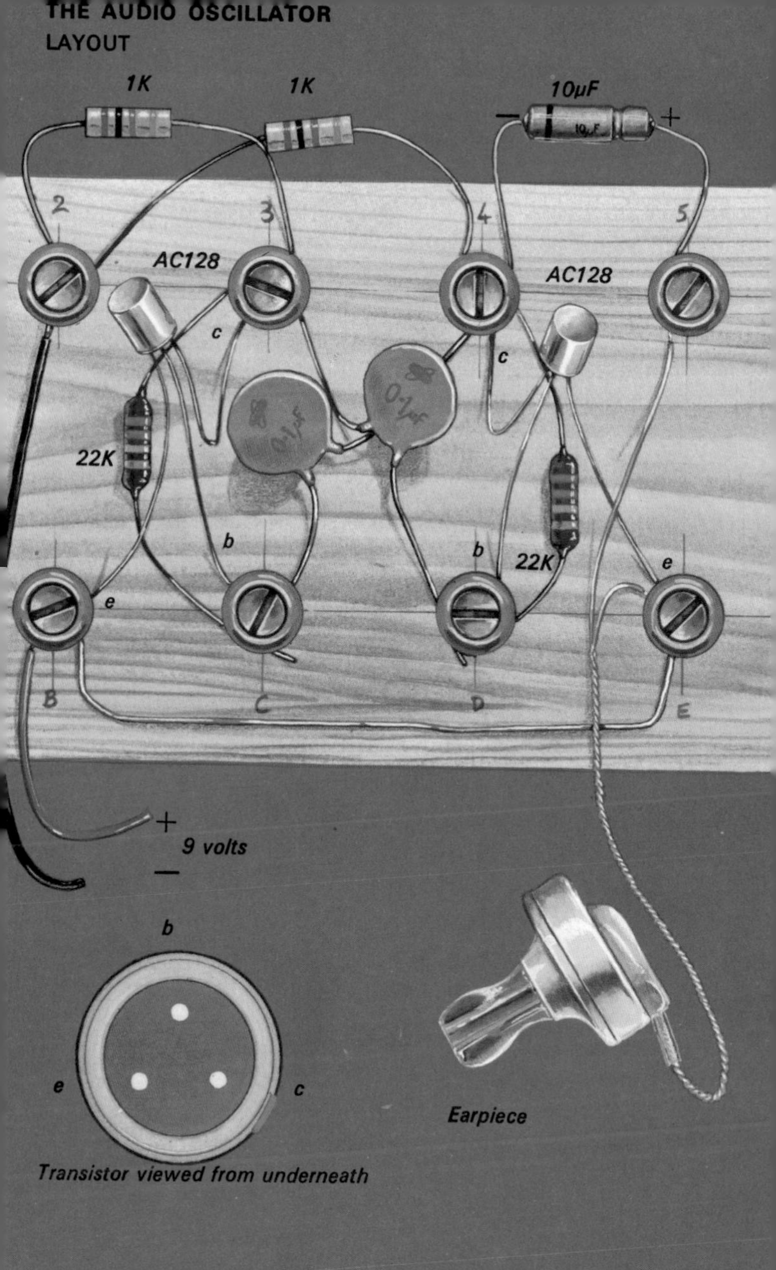
THE AUDIO OSCILLATOR
LAYOUT
1K
1K
10µF
AC128
AC128
22K
22K
c
c
b
b
e
e
2
3
4
5
B
C
D
E
+
9 volts
—
b
e
c
Transistor viewed from underneath
Earpiece

Morse code oscillator

It is possible to send messages in morse code using the audio oscillator. Touching one of the battery leads on and off its connection will produce ‘bleeps’. If the correct order of long and short bleeps is produced, this will be a morse code message.

In order to send morse code, a morse *key* is required. This is a fast on-off switch which can be pressed down for on and will then spring off. You may have your own morse key (‘tapper’ is the wrong word!), or a door bell push button can be used. If not, it is simple to make a morse key from a piece of tin plate.

How to make the morse key is shown in the drawing. It can be made from a piece of tin plate cut from a tin lid, cut to size with tinsnips or large scissors. Tin plate is VERY SHARP, so it is wise to ask an adult to do this job. The tin plate is bent to the shape shown. Knock a small hole in the end with a nail, resting the tin plate on an old piece of wood and then screw on a piece of scrap wood as a handle.

The morse key acts as a switch in the positive (+) battery lead, with a connection from B to 1 – the morse key switching across A to 1. Two extra components are added to the earpiece output circuit: a 4.7K resistor and a 0.1 μF capacitor. These act as a filter for the sound and get rid of its harsh tone.

The modified circuit diagram and layout show how the morse code oscillator is built. Connect the battery. If you press the key down in the correct way you will be able to send morse messages.

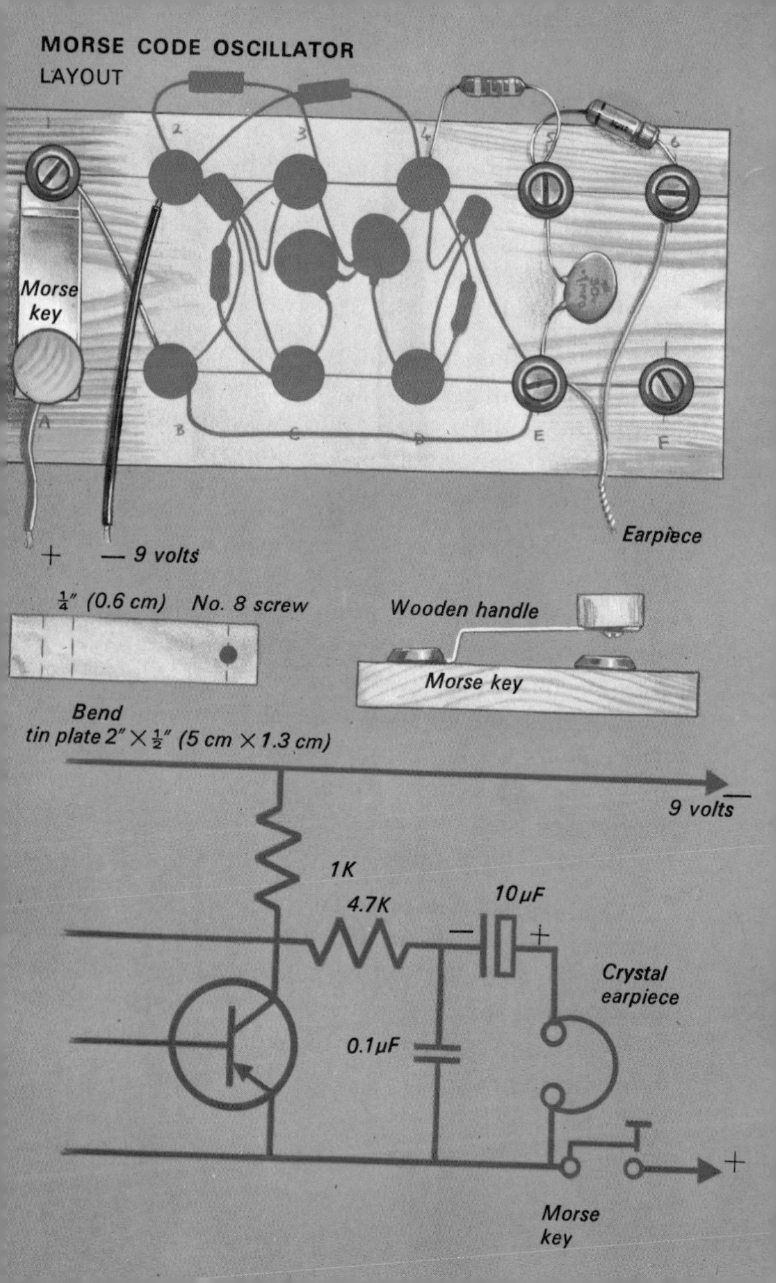
MORSE CODE OSCILLATOR
LAYOUT
Morse key
A
B
C
D
E
F
1
2
3
4
5
6
+
— 9 volts
Earpiece
¼" (0.6 cm)
No. 8 screw
Bend
tin plate 2" × ½" (5 cm × 1.3 cm)
Wooden handle
Morse key
9 volts —
1K
4.7K
10μF
— +
Crystal
earpiece
0.1μF
Morse
key
+

A two-way morse station

The morse code oscillator is useful for practising the morse code, but can only be heard by one person at a time. The real purpose of morse is communication: being in contact with someone else. True communication also goes two ways, so the simple morse code oscillator would be better as a two-way morse station.

A two-way morse system is shown in the layout diagram. The morse code oscillator becomes the main station and another small board, called the *slave station*, is also built. This simply places another morse key and earpiece on the end of a three-lead cable.

The board for the slave station is made up as shown with four screwcups to hold the key and earpiece. The two stations are connected using a length of three-core electric mains lead, the sort of wire that might go from the plug to a television or lamp. Three-core 5 amp is the lightest and cheapest and will do the job very well. The colours of the lead are shown in the drawing to make the connections easier to follow. The second morse key and earpiece are connected 'across' the main ones. This is called connecting *in parallel*.

When the two-way system is made up, pressing down either of the keys will produce a sound in both earpieces. Using this system it will be possible to send messages across a room or from room to room in the morse code. All that has to be learned is the morse code and how to send morse messages.

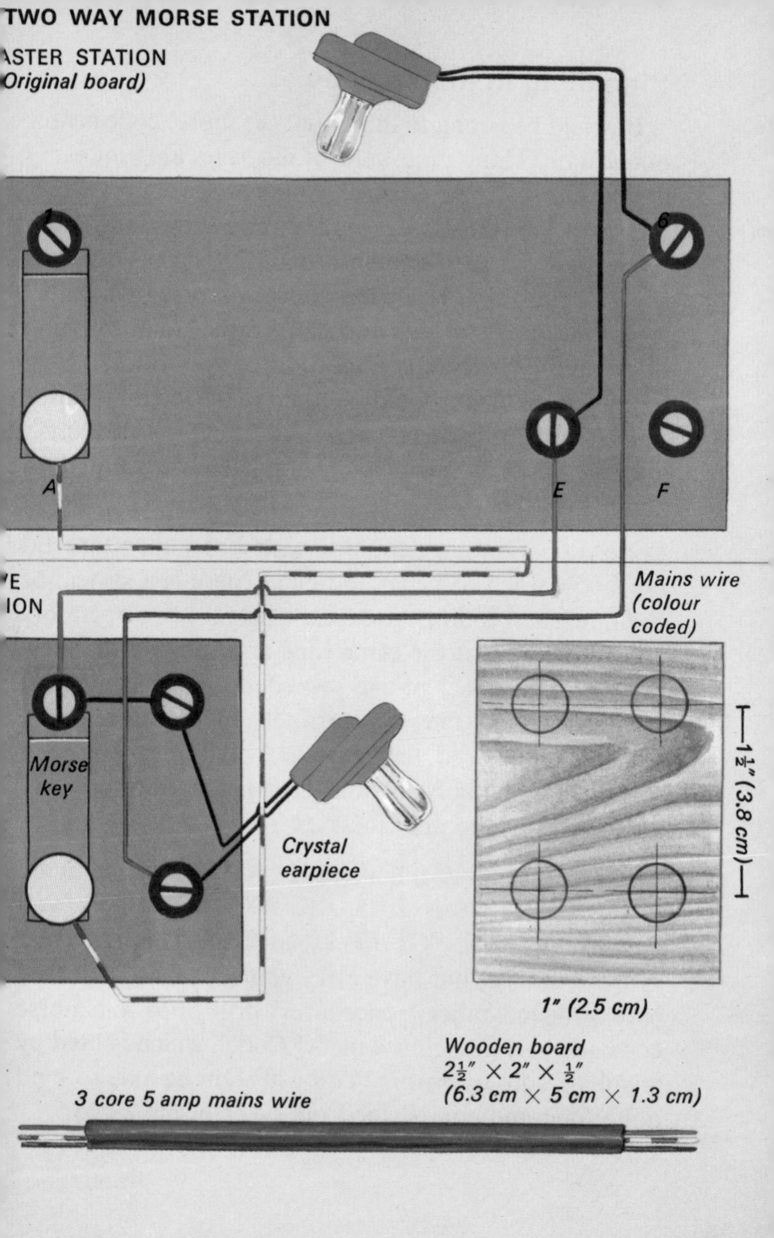

TWO WAY MORSE STATION
ASTER STATION
Original board)
1
6
A
E
F
Morse key
Crystal earpiece
Mains wire (colour coded)
1½" (3.8 cm)
1" (2.5 cm)
Wooden board
2½" × 2" × ½"
(6.3 cm × 5 cm × 1.3 cm)
3 core 5 amp mains wire

Signalling in morse code

It would be wrong to think that the morse code is now out of date. Many thousands of messages are sent every day in morse. Some are from ships at sea, but weather messages, news messages and several thousand Radio 'Hams' use morse to send information. The basic code is shown opposite. It is simpler to learn morse by memorising the sounds of 'dits and dahs' rather than thinking of dot dash. Spacing is important in good morse code sending. One 'dah' should be equal to the length of three 'dits', the space between two letters equal to three 'dits', and the space between two complete words equal to about five 'dits'.

No proper message could be sent if the operators did not know when to begin and end. There is a system of beginning and ending messages so that the two operators are not sending at the same time and spoiling the message. This is called morse *procedure signals*, and here are the simplest ones to learn. Begin the message by sending CT – send the message – AR means end of message – sending K, invites the other station to begin. At the end of the final message send VA.

A simple message might read: "CT What is the time? AR K". "CT It is 1045 AR K". "CT Thank you goodbye VA K". "CT Goodbye VA". This is only a simple example, but have a try yourself; it is great fun. You will find other 'procedures' in a book on morse code and also how to use the 'Q Code', which is used by amateur radio operators. You will soon be able to send quite long and complicated messages in morse.

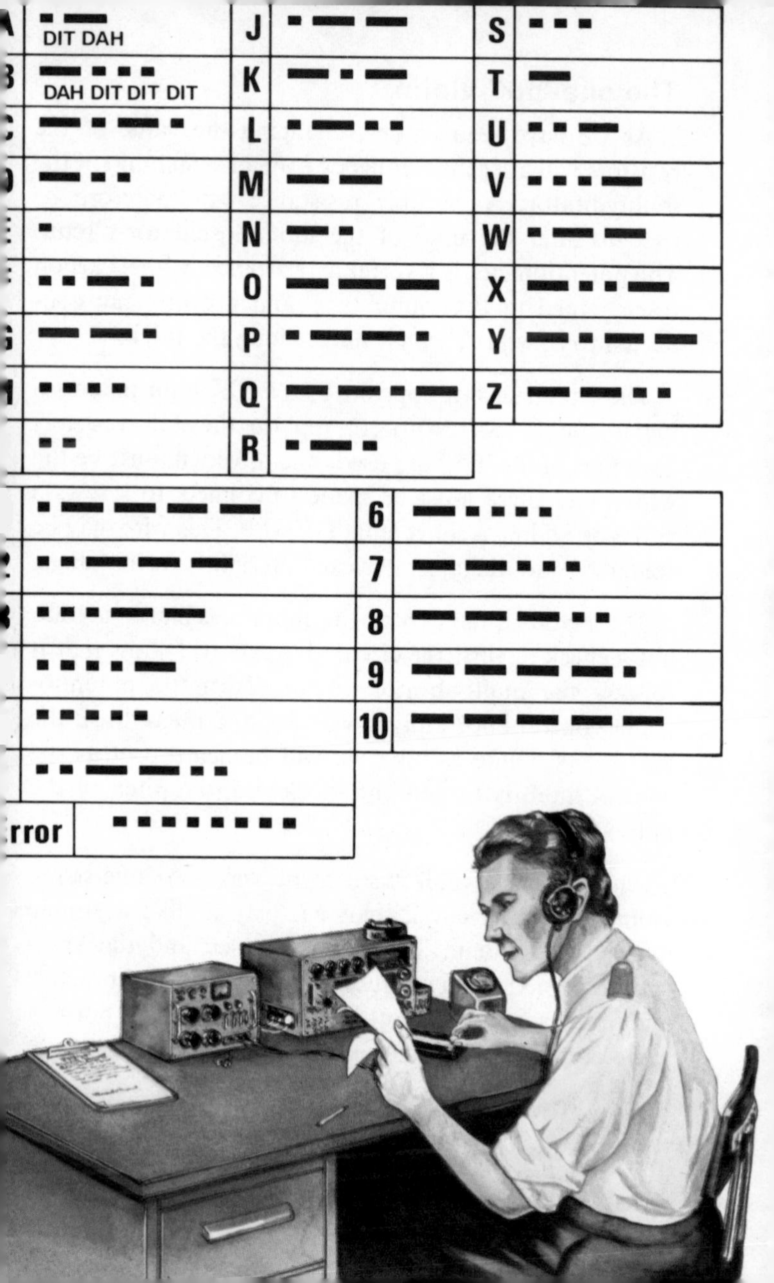

DIT DAH
DAH DIT DIT DIT
J
K
L
M
N
O
P
Q
R
S
T
U
V
W
X
Y
Z
6
7
8
9
10

The one 'pot' violin

As we have seen earlier, changing the value of the resistors will alter the frequency (rate of switching) of the multivibrator. A variable resistance can therefore be used to alter the note of the morse oscillator circuit. The potentiometer is a variable resistance, with a carbon track joined to two outer tags, and a centre tag connected to a 'wiper', which slides along the track.

The circuit shown opposite uses a 50K ohm potentiometer and a 1K resistor to replace the 22K resistor. Two tags of the 'pot' are used, one of which must be the wiper, and these must be made to connect to screws 5 and 6 by adding a short length of wire. This wire may be soldered onto the tags or twisted on tightly, using pliers.

The layout differs from the morse oscillator layout, but a check against the circuit diagram will show that it follows the multivibrator circuit. Turn the potentiometer control knob fully clockwise, and press down the morse key. Quite a low note will be heard, but as the control knob is turned anti-clockwise, the pitch of the note will rise.

An old music hall instrument was the 'one-string violin', and this circuit can be 'played' like a simple musical instrument. The key is pressed and the knob can be turned to give musical notes; a bit of practice and you have a one 'pot' violin. Later in the book a more complex electronic organ will be built.

ONE 'POT' VIOLIN

LAYOUT

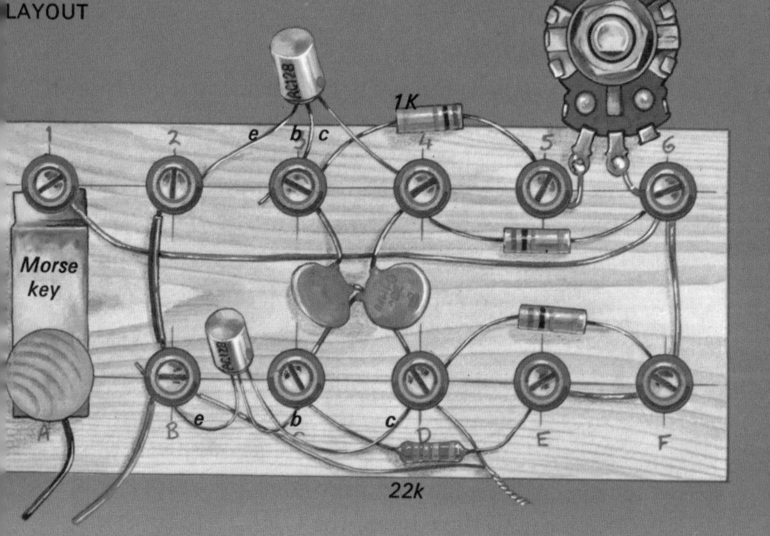

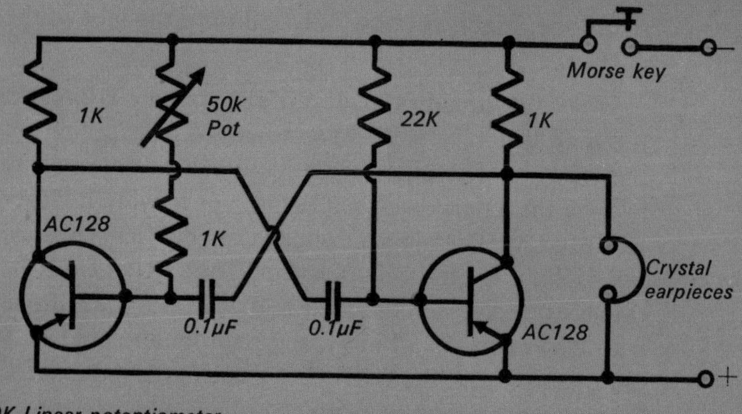

50K Linear potentiometer

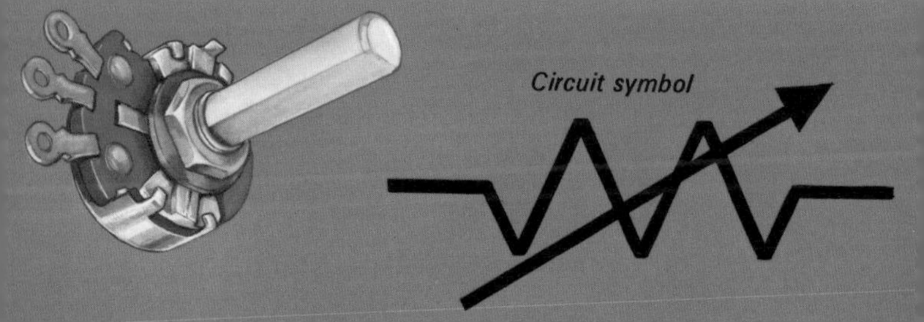

The photophon

The *photophon* is a novelty circuit using a component called a *light dependent resistor*, or cadmium-sulphide cell. Cadmium-sulphide is a chemical which changes resistance with the amount of light allowed to fall on it. The ORP 12 L.D.R. (light dependent resistor) has a resistance which varies from several thousand ohms in darkness to a few ohms in strong light.

The 1K resistor of the previous circuit is replaced by a 10K resistor and the potentiometer is replaced by the ORP 12. The change in layout is shown. The operation of the ORP 12 can be spoiled by light coming in the side of its casing. This may be prevented by wrapping black PVC tape round the edge of the ORP 12 to form a light-tight tube. Light will now only fall onto the face of the ORP 12.

When the circuit is made up and the key is pressed the note will vary with the amount of light falling on the ORP 12. The pitch of the note can be changed by passing the hands over the ORP 12, or moving it closer to a window. The range of pitch is smaller than the 'one pot violin', but the circuit is fun. The ORP 12 can be rather expensive, so unless the reader wishes to continue with electronics as a hobby, the photophon could be a luxury. However, the ORP 12 is a useful component for future electronic experiments.

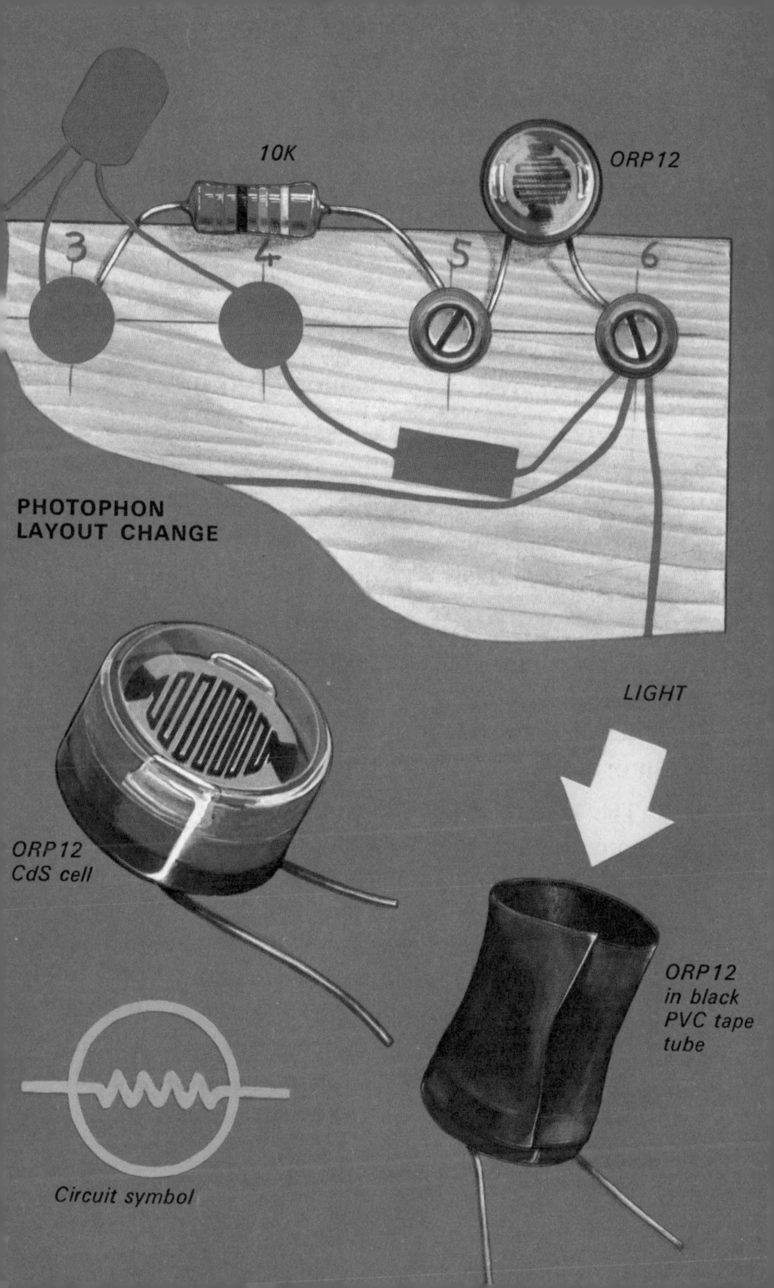
10K
ORP12
3
4
5
6
PHOTOPHON
LAYOUT CHANGE
LIGHT
ORP12
CdS cell
ORP12
in black
PVC tape
tube
Circuit symbol

Simple electronic organ
1 Basic circuit and layout

In the 'one pot violin' and the 'photophon' the base resistor was varied to alter the pitch of the note produced by the audio oscillator – we were making musical notes by electronics. If it were possible to switch these 'electronic notes' in musical steps, a different note in a musical scale being played each time a switch is pushed, we would have a simple electronic organ.

One way of doing this would be to build a lot of audio oscillators, each one tuned to its own musical note. A far easier (and less expensive) method is to build one audio oscillator and switch in different values of resistance to produce a range of notes from one circuit.

The circuit to do this is shown opposite. It is like the 'one pot violin', but the potentiometer is replaced by a series of resistors which vary in 'steps' to produce a series of notes. These steps will be switched to act like an organ keyboard.

The layout of the audio oscillator shows that this circuit is built onto a larger circuit board which will allow space for an amplifier stage to be added later. The new board is an 8in (20cm) length of the $2\frac{3}{4}$in $\times$ $\frac{1}{2}$in (7cm $\times$ 1.3cm) wood used to build the original circuit board. This board holds 16 screws and screwcups, spaced in the same way as the original 12 screws. The circuit is built up as shown, in the same careful way as the earlier circuits. Two wires will go from the screws marked A and B to the *keyboard*, which will be built on another piece of wood.

SIMPLE ELECTRONIC ORGAN

CIRCUIT

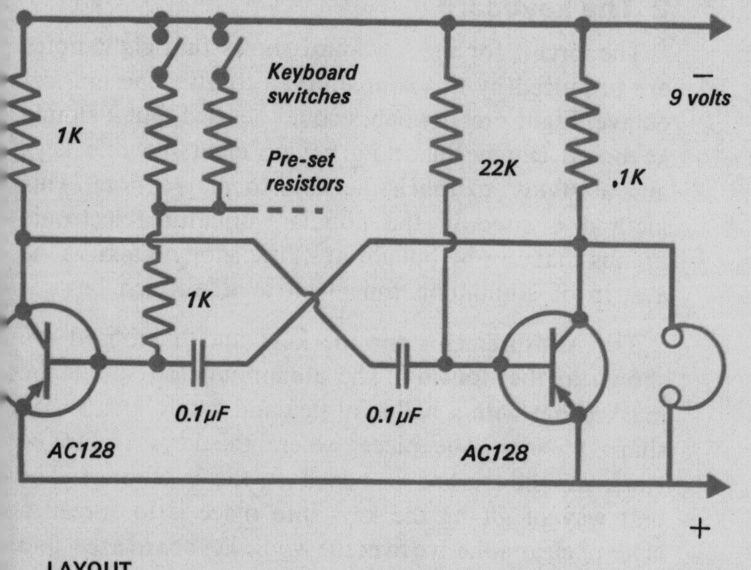

LAYOUT

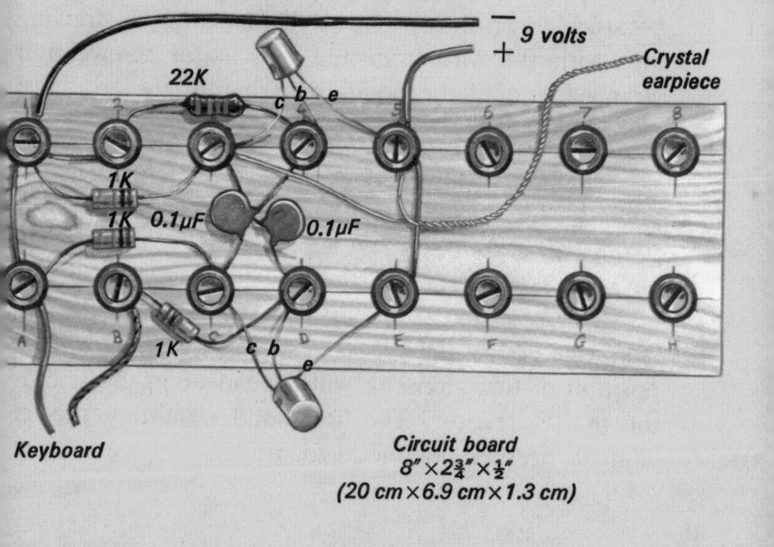

Simple electronic organ
2 The keyboard

The circuit for the keyboard shows that eight notes are produced by this simple organ to give one musical octave. Eight press switches could be used, but a simple keyboard can be made by having eight metallic keys and a 'stylus' to touch the keys to play a note. This method is used in the popular miniature electronic organs that can be bought at music shops. Each key is a strip of aluminium foil glued to a wooden base.

The measurements for the keys and baseboard are shown in the drawing. The aluminium foil should be marked out with a ballpoint pen and carefully cut with sharp scissors. The places where the keys are to be stuck can be marked in pencil on the baseboard. The best way of gluing the keys into place is to spread a layer of clear adhesive over the whole keyboard area, and firmly press each key into place. The whole key should be stuck down firmly. The stylus is simply a drawing pin, with the wire from audio oscillator screwcup B wrapped around the point, pushed into the end of a piece of wooden dowelling rod.

Each note is tuned by a *pre-set resistor* – a small potentiometer which is adjusted by a screwdriver. A No. 8 screwcup and screw is placed at the top of each key, this is connected to the 'wiper' tag of the pre-set resistor. A second screwcup (No. 8) connects the tag from one end of the pre-set resistor carbon track. The position of this screwcup will depend upon the size of the pre-set resistor. The horizontal mounting pre-set controls are best for the keyboard.

KEYBOARD CIRCUIT

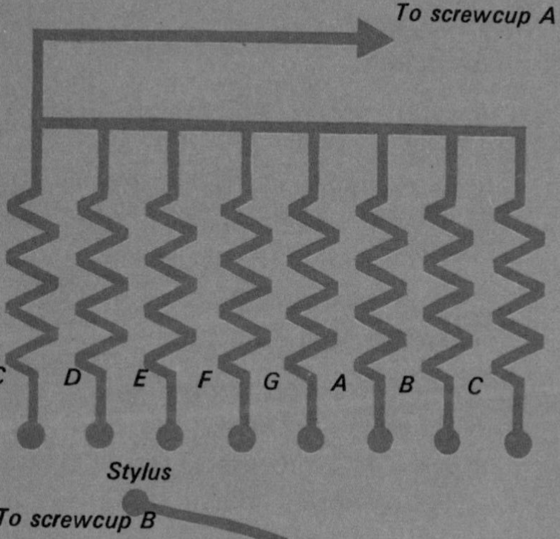

To screwcup A

C D E F G A B C

Stylus

To screwcup B

$\frac{3}{8}$" (1 cm) dowel
2" (5 cm) long

KEYBOARD

To screwcup A

Stylus

PVC covered wire to screwcup B

Eight 50K or 47K pre-set resistors

wire wrapped around drawing pin pushed into dowel

No. 8 screws and screwcups

'wiper' tag

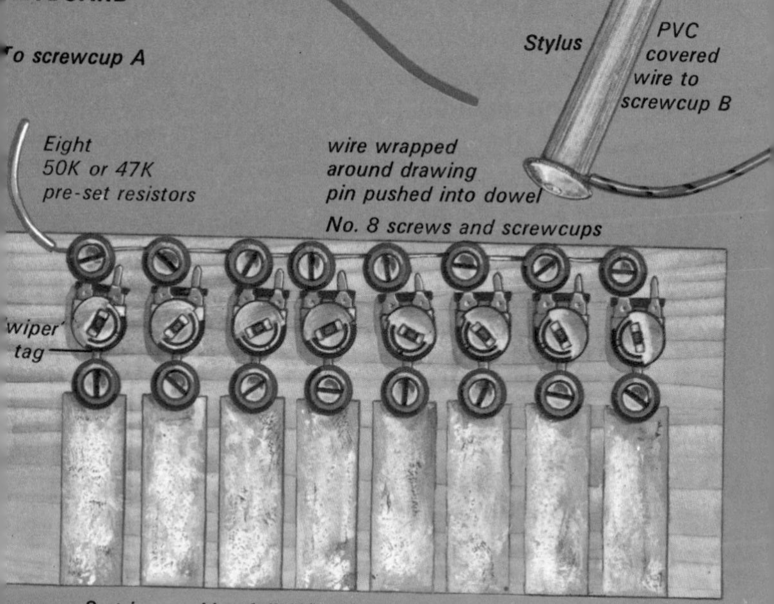

8 strips cooking foil $1\frac{1}{2}" \times \frac{1}{2}"$ (3.8 cm × 1.3 cm) $\frac{1}{8}"$ (0.3 cm) apart

Baseboard $6" \times 2\frac{3}{4}" \times \frac{1}{2}"$ (15 cm × 6.9 cm × 1.3 cm)

Simple electronic organ
3 Tuning the keyboard

The illustrated keyboard shows miniature horizontal mounting pre-sets, but if these are not available, vertical mounting pre-sets can be used. These are usually larger, with 3 tags at the bottom. The centre tag and one of the end tags are bent up so that they can be mounted under two No. 8 screwcups as shown. This requires care, as the tags are close together. Cut off the unused tag.

The organ can be tuned to notes from the C above 'Middle C' upwards on a piano. Connect the stylus and the wire which joins up all the pre-sets to screws B and A on the audio oscillator board. When the stylus is placed onto a key, a note will be produced. The pianist plays the C above 'Middle C' and the extreme left pre-set is adjusted until that key plays the same note. The next note is played and the next pre-set adjusted, and so on until all the keys are in tune. This organ is 'monotonic', that is, it will only play one correct note at once. If the stylus touches two keys, one out-of-tune note will be produced.

Although pre-set controls are much better, it is possible to tune the notes with fixed resistors, but it is not possible to get the correct values to tune each required note. However, with a little care, fixed resistor values can be changed by filing carefully into the carbon film inside the casing. This makes the resistance increase. This operation is difficult because the resistor must be filed slowly (as shown), while the note is being played, until the pitch is correct. File 12K resistors for the top four notes and 22K resistors for the bottom four notes.

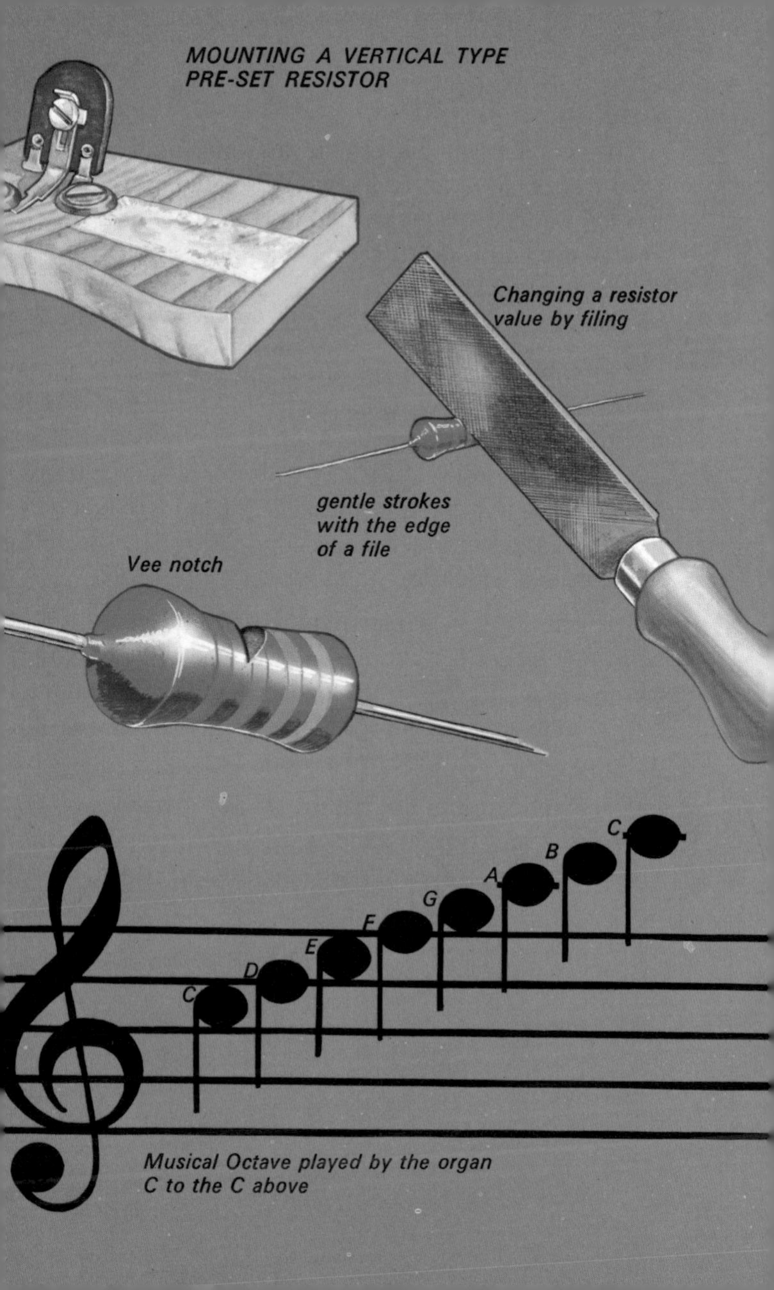
MOUNTING A VERTICAL TYPE
PRE-SET RESISTOR
Changing a resistor
value by filing
gentle strokes
with the edge
of a file
Vee notch
C
D
E
F
G
A
B
C
Musical Octave played by the organ
C to the C above

Adding an amplifier

The simple organ built so far has only enough volume to supply an earpiece. To increase the volume an *amplifier* has to be added. We have used the transistor as a switch and an oscillator, but it can also amplify, that is, make signals louder. This action of the transistor is explained on page 28 of *Making a Transistor Radio*.

The circuit diagram for the amplifier stage is illustrated opposite. The note comes from the organ, through a capacitor (10μF) into the base of the transistor. The amplified note appears at the collector where a transformer feeds it into a loudspeaker. The loudspeaker acts like the earpiece and changes the electrical note into sound waves which are quite loud.

The output transformer required is the Eagle LT700 and the loudspeaker should be of a type between 3 and 8 ohms. A small 3in (7.5cm) loudspeaker is very suitable, but to save cost a loudspeaker salvaged from an old radio or television set can be used.

The amplifier does not require its own battery supply. It is connected to the battery supply used to power the audio oscillator. When the amplifier is added more battery power is used so a large PP9 battery will last longer than the small PP3.

AMPLIFIER

CIRCUIT DIAGRAM

—

olts

LT700
Transformer

33K

Loudspeaker
3–8 Ω

om
gan

10μF

AC128

10K

1K

+

100μF

+

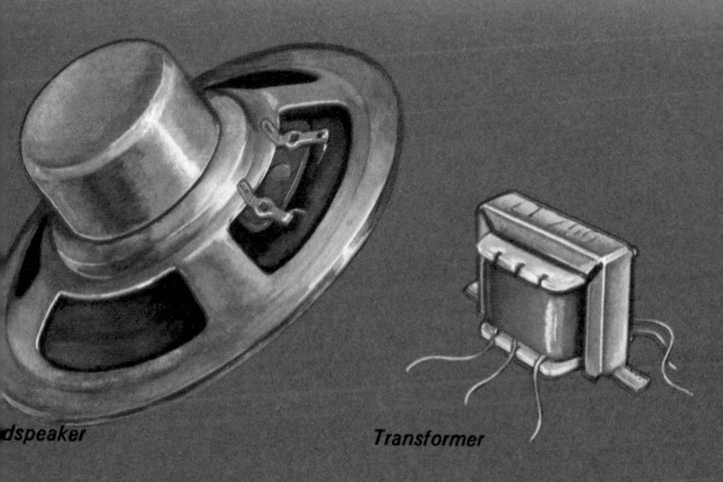

Building the amplifier

The layout drawing shows the amplifier stage mounted on the spare screwcups on the right of the audio oscillator board. The LT700 transformer must be mounted the correct way round. One side of the transformer has two leads – these are connected to 8 and H for the loudspeaker output. The other side has three leads; the centre lead is not required and can be removed, and the other two leads are joined to 7 and G.

The 10μF capacitor has a rather difficult and long path between screws 3 and 6. Although it will only just reach across between the screws, it must not touch any of the leads around screws 4 and 5. It is helpful to cut two lengths of PVC sleeving off some PVC covered wire to slip over the bare leads of this capacitor to insulate it from screws 4 and 5. Both capacitors must be mounted the correct way round. It may also be helpful to place some lengths of PVC sleeving on the transistor leads for the amplifier and oscillator, but ensure that *bare* wire is trapped under the screwcups to make a good connection.

When the amplifier has been wired up, connect the battery and try the keyboard. Quite loud notes, enough to fill a room, will be heard from the speaker. Remember to disconnect the battery after playing the organ. Although no sound can be heard when the stylus is not touching a key, the organ is still using battery power until it is disconnected. A small switch could be fitted in the + battery lead.

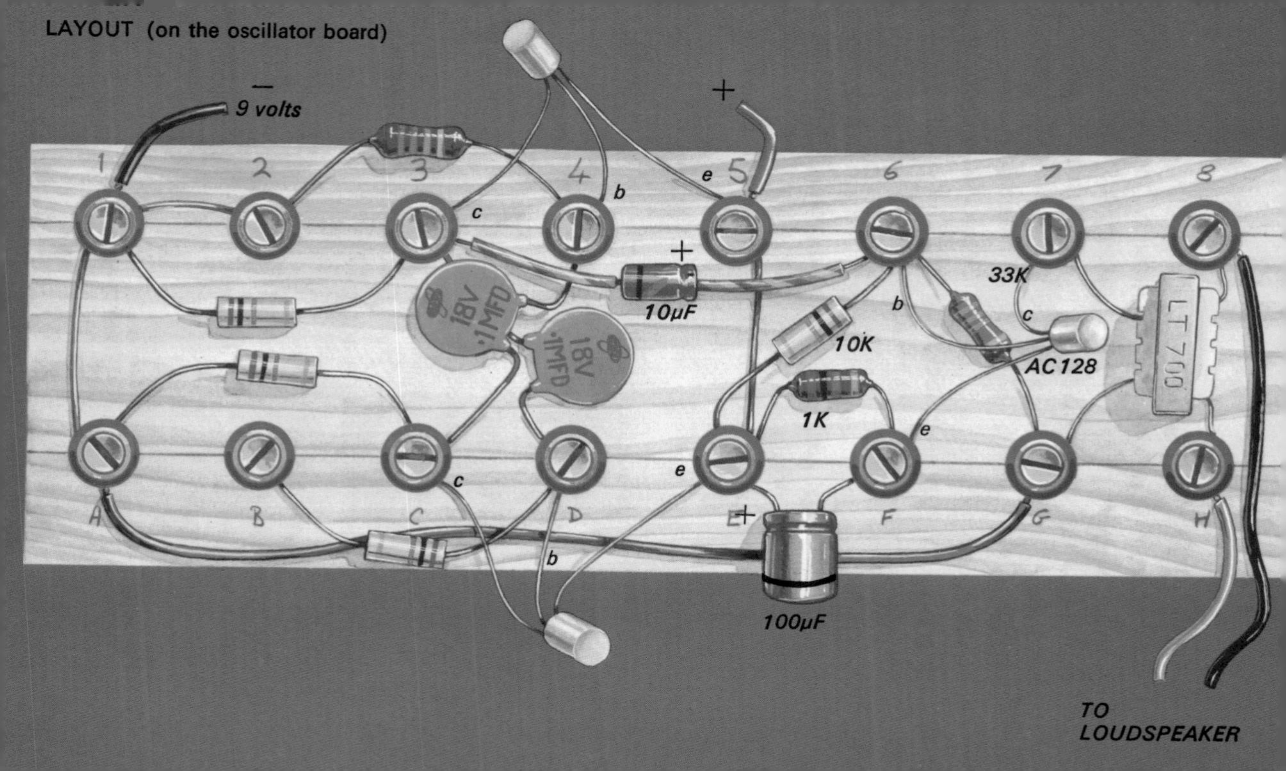

LAYOUT (on the oscillator board)
–
9 volts
+
1
2
3
4
5
6
7
8
A
B
C
D
E+
F
G
H
c
b
e
18V ·1MFD
18V ·1MFD
10μF
10K
1K
33K
AC128
LT 700
100μF
TO LOUDSPEAKER

A vibrato circuit

The organ built so far will produce reasonably clear notes, but they are rather 'flat' in tone, in comparison with a normal electronic organ. Most electronic organs have some form of *vibrato* added to the note. This is a sort of 'tremble' which gives the characteristic electronic organ sound. There are several circuits which could produce a vibrato note, including the flip-flop which we have used throughout this book.

A suitable circuit for a vibrato oscillator is shown opposite. The values of resistor and capacitor have been chosen to produce a gentle vibration to add to the notes. The output of the vibrato is fed, via a capacitor and resistor, to the collector of the oscillator board transistor which leads to the amplifier (screw 3).

The vibrato is built up as shown in the layout drawing, using the same careful method of construction. The output and battery leads are arranged to come out of the same side of the board so that they may be conveniently connected to the oscillator board. The battery – lead goes to oscillator board screw 1, and the + lead goes to screw 5. A switch link between screws 6 and F is included. This link may be replaced by a switch to switch the vibrato effect on and off.

The three boards, oscillator, keyboard and vibrato, may now be connected together to give a one-octave organ which is capable of playing simple tunes, and is all your own work.

VIBRATO

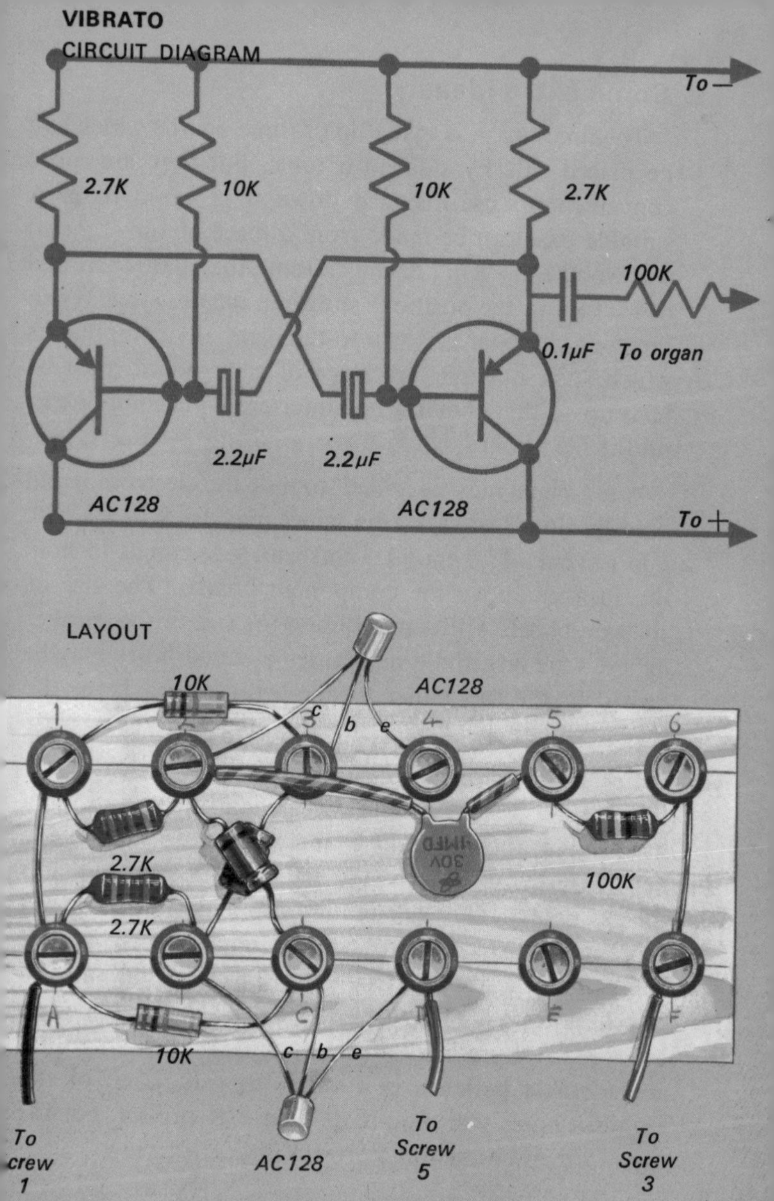
CIRCUIT DIAGRAM
2.7K
10K
10K
2.7K
To —
100K
0.1µF
To organ
2.2µF
2.2µF
AC128
AC128
To +
LAYOUT
10K
AC128
c
b
e
1
2
3
4
5
6
2.7K
2.7K
100K
30V
4MFD
A
C
E
F
10K
c
b
e
To
crew
1
AC128
To
Screw
5
To
Screw
3

Some extra ideas

The final organ is made up of three boards which can be placed side by side on a table, but they are more convenient to use fastened down to a wood base. A suitable base can be made from a piece of $\frac{1}{2}$ in (1.3 cm) soft wood 8 in × 8 in (20 cm × 20 cm), the boards screwed down to it in the positions shown in the drawing. When screwing the boards down to the base, any components which stick out over the edge of each board must be bent up so that they do not interfere with components on the next board.

A top panel may be added, to hide the electronics and hold the loudspeaker. This panel may be 8 in × 7 in × $\frac{1}{2}$ in (20 cm × 17.5 cm × 1.3 cm) with side panels to hold the speaker above the component boards. The size of the side panels will depend upon the size of the speaker in use. One large hole or a series of small holes may be drilled in the top panel to allow the sound from the speaker to escape.

For constructors who fancy going further with their organ, it is possible to tune the oscillator up to one and a half octaves above Middle C. It is also possible to include keys to give the sharps and flats of this range (piano 'black' notes). This will require the making of a much more complex keyboard (shown opposite) from foil. The 'white' notes could be 1 in (2.5 cm) wide and the 'black' notes $\frac{1}{2}$ in (1.3cm) wide. A clear gap must be left between each individual note, and this will require considerable patience in cutting the foil. Each of the eighteen notes will require its own 47K pre-set, but for the more ambitious, this project is worth trying.

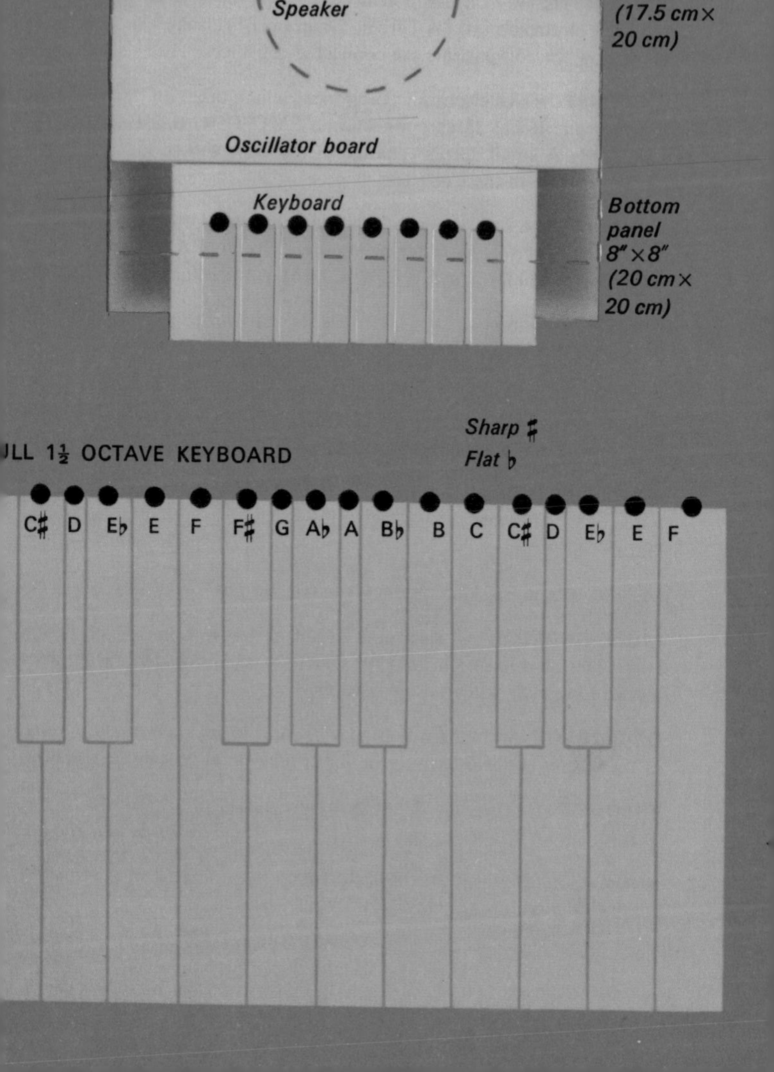

SSIBLE
RGAN
OUNTING
Vibrato board
Speaker
Oscillator board
Keyboard
Top panel
7″×8″
(17.5 cm×
20 cm)
Bottom
panel
8″×8″
(20 cm×
20 cm)
LL 1½ OCTAVE KEYBOARD
Sharp ♯
Flat ♭
C♯ D E♭ E F F♯ G A♭ A B♭ B C C♯ D E♭ E F

GLOSSARY OF TERMS

COMPONENTS The "parts" used to make a piece of electronic equipment.

CIRCUIT The way the components are wired together to perform the required electronic task. A Circuit Diagram is a "map" or "plan" to show how the components are connected together.

TRANSISTOR An electronic component which takes an "active" part in a circuit. It has three connections: EMITTER, BASE and COLLECTOR. A small current change in the Base will produce a larger current change in the Collector.

CAPACITOR A component which allows an electronic signal to pass, but not the fixed voltages which power a circuit. CAPACITANCE is measured in small units of a FARAD, called microfarads (*u*F).

RESISTOR A component which "resists" or tries to prevent, the flow of current in a circuit. RESISTANCE is measured in OHMS.

POTENTIOMETER A variable resistance which has a carbon track connected to two outer contacts; an inner contact goes to a wiper arm which makes contact on the required part of the carbon resistance track.

LIGHT DEPENDENT RESISTOR (L.D.R.) A component, the resistance of which varies according to the amount of light shining on its "face."

SERIES A number of components wired "in line".

MULTIVIBRATOR An electronic circuit of two sections, which switch each other on and off. A FLIP-FLOP (or Astable Multivibrator) does this continuously when power is applied.

OSCILLATOR A circuit which goes "round in its own circle". Some of the output is put back into the input to maintain the cycle of action.

FREQUENCY The number of complete cycles of oscillation in one second.

AUDIO Sounds which can be detected by the human ear. Audio Frequency Oscillations are oscillations which we can hear.